1,000

HELPFUL
ADJECTIVES
for fiction writers

VALERIE HOWARD

CONTENTS

INTRODUCTION

HAVE YOU ever struggled to describe something in your book because you couldn't pin down the perfect adjective? Sometimes going beyond the "good," the "bad," and the "ugly" can be difficult, but never fear, your handy book of helpful adjectives is here! Before we dive in, here are some tips for boosting an adjective's effectiveness:

Be unpredictable. Using an unexpected adjective can be powerful. Instead of saying the little girl in your story is "frail" or "delicate" as everyone would describe her, say she's "papery" or "see-through." Reach into the recesses of your mind to find an unusual way to describe your noun.

Be accurate. Is the object you're writing about just plain "small" or is it "minuscule," "tiny," or "shrunken" instead? Is your character "mopey," "sullen," or "nonchalant"? Switching out the adjective can alter the meaning of the sentence. It's up to you—the author—to choose which word fits your story best.

Alliterate (sparingly). Using alliteration well can

give a musical quality to your writing. Instead of giving your character a "bulky handbag," try a "hulking handbag." Hear the difference? (Don't overdo it. If you alliterate every adjective/noun pair, you run the risk of repulsing rapt readers.)

Avoid "very." You know you're using a droopy adjective when you have to stuff a "very" into your sentence to fill it out. Instead of "very large," say "gigantic" or "looming."

Avoid a long list of adjectives. That move will make your writing boring, dull, tedious, dry, and bland. (Not to mention, kind of annoying.)

If you're still struggling to find the right adjective to describe your noun, remember that most verbs can be magically transformed into adjectives by adding a suffix like "-ing" or "-ed." Ask yourself, "What happened to this object?" Did someone shred it? Try "shredded." Did it freeze? Try "frozen" or "freezing."

I've grouped these adjectives by the type of noun they describe, such as size, opacity, or quality. There is also a space at the end of this book to write in your own favorite adjectives so you can have those words right at your fingertips.

Happy writing! I wish you great success. If you need to contact me, my info is on the back page.

Affluence

Poor

Destitute
Humble
Impoverished
Low-class
Modest
Needy

Rich

Affluent
Deluxe
Elegant
Extravagant
Exuberant
Lavish
Luxurious
Opulent
Posh
Prosperous
Ritzy
Swanky
Wealthy
Well-to-do

AGE

New

    Cutting edge
    Fresh
    Modern
    State of the art

Old

    Aged
    Ancient
    Elderly
    Grizzled
    Mature
    Past one's prime
    Ripened
    Seasoned
    Vintage

Young

    Babyish
    Budding
    Fledgling
    Inexperienced
    Newborn
    Tender

Attractiveness

Attractive

Adorable
Alluring
Appealing
Bewitching
Captivating
Charming
Cuddly
Cunning
Cute
Darling
Enticing
Huggable
Irresistible
Magnetic
Precious
Sweet
Tantalizing
Tempting
Winsome

Repulsive

Disgusting
Gross
Nauseating

Obscene
Repugnant
Revolting
Sickening

Shocked
Stunned
Stupefied

Upset

Crabby
Cranky
Cross
Dour
Fussy
Grumpy
Huffy
Sullen
Touchy

HEIGHT & LENGTH

Short

Abbreviated
Brief
Clipped
Concise
Cut
Ground-hugging
Low
Snipped
Squat
Stumpy
Stunted
Trimmed
Truncated

Tall

Alpine
Elevated
Lanky
Lofty
Looming
Mountainous
Soaring
Towering

Long

Elongated
Enlarged
Expanded
Extended
Lengthened
Prolonged
Stretched out
Stringy

OPACITY

Semi-Opaque

Blurry
Cloudy
Filmy
Foggy
Gauzy
Hazy
Misty
Muddy
Murky
Semitransparent
Smoggy
Smokey
Soupy

See-Through

Clear
Gossamer
Sheer
Translucent
Transparent
Vaporous

Personality Trait

Annoying

    Bothersome
    Galling
    Grating
    Irritating
    Nettlesome
    Pesky
    Pestering

Brave

    Adventuresome
    Bold
    Courageous
    Daring
    Fearless
    Gallant
    Heroic

Boring

    Drab
    Dry
    Dull
    Tedious
    Tiresome

Childish

Immature
Infantile
Juvenile

Clumsy

Accident-prone
Bumbling
Butterfingered
Inept
Klutzy

Energetic

Bustling
Frisky
Lively
Spirited
Sprightly
Spry
Vigorous

Friendly

Accommodating
Affable
Amiable
Approachable
Benevolent

Bubbly
Charitable
Chummy
Congenial
Considerate
Cooperative
Doting
Easy-going
Fond
Generous
Gracious
Hospitable
Obliging
Polite
Sociable
Soft
Tender
Warm

Indecisive

Fickle
Inconsistent
Volatile

Laid-back

Blasé
Carefree
Casual
Easygoing

Freewheeling
Indifferent
Irresponsible
Nonchalant

Likable

Admirable
Enviable
Ideal
Laudable
Popular
Praiseworthy
Respectable
Revered

Mean

Abusive
Acidic
Aggressive
Back-stabbing
Belligerent
Biting
Bitter
Brutal
Cantankerous
Catty
Churlish
Combative
Cruel

Smart

Brainy
Brilliant
Clever
Ingenious
Keen
Omniscient
Savvy
Sharp
Shrewd
Streetwise
Wise

Strange

Aberrant
Abnormal
Awkward
Bizarre
Creepy
Demented
Deranged
Eccentric
Freakish
Goofy
Mutant
Peculiar
Psychotic
Unconventional
Unnatural

Unsettling
Unusual

Stupid

Absurd
Asinine
Dense
Gullible
Idiotic
Ludicrous
Moronic
Naive
Obtuse
Outrageous
Preposterous
Simple

Suspicious

Discreet
Guarded
Heedful
Prudent
Vigilant
Wary

Talented

Accomplished
Adept
Deft
Experienced
Expert
Learned
Polished
Skilled

Other

Arrogant
Bored
Vain

Physical Appearance

Beautiful

Breathtaking
Dapper
Gorgeous
Radiant
Snazzy
Sophisticated
Stunning
Stylish

Distorted

Askew
Bedraggled
Contorted
Crooked
Deformed
Dilapidated
Discolored
Disheveled
Faded
Gnarled
Grainy
Intertwined
Mangled
Misshapen

PLIABILITY

Pliable

Agile
Bendable
Bouncy
Chewy
Elastic
Flexible
Limber
Malleable
Moldable
Nimble
Springy
Stretchy
Yielding

Not Pliable

Brittle
Fixed
Hard-and-fast
Immobile
Impenetrable
Impermeable
Rigid
Sound
Steely

Stiff
Stringent
Sturdy
Tense
Tight
Uncompromising
Unyielding
Wooden

SIZE

Small

Bitty
Diminutive
Dinky
Dwarfish
Microscopic
Miniature
Minuscule
Petite
Pint-sized
Pocket-sized
Puny
Runty
Shrimpy
Shriveled
Shrunken
Slight
Teeny
Tiny
Wee

Medium

Average
Mid-sized
Moderate

Large

Astronomical
Galactic
Gargantuan
Gigantic
Hulking
Mammoth
Massive
Over-sized
Roomy
Spacious
Titanic
Vast
Voluminous
Whopping

Thick

Broad
Bulbous
Bulging
Bulky
Caked
Chubby
Chunky
Congealed
Deep
Fat
Husky
Obese

Paunchy
Plump
Potbellied
Pudgy
Roly-poly
Shapely
Stocky
Stubby
Substantial
Swollen
Tubby
Wide

Thin

Bony
Delicate
Emaciated
Fine
Flat
Fragile
Gangly
Gaunt
Lean
Narrow
Papery
Scrawny
Skeletal
Skinny
Sleek
Slender

Slim
Spindly
Squished
Svelte
Threadlike
Trim
Wan
Willowy
Wiry
Wispy

Sound

Loud

Blaring
Blasting
Booming
Clamorous
Deafening
Earsplitting
Piercing
Resounding
Roaring
Thunderous

Quiet

Calm
Hushed
Inaudible
Muted
Silent
Soundless
Subdued
Tinny
Tranquil
Whispered

Specific

Crackling
Creaky
Grinding
Raspy
Ringing
Screeching
Shrill
Whirring

SPEED

Fast

    Accelerated
Breakneck
Brisk
Expedited
Fleet
Galloping
Hasty
Hurried
Rapid
Speedy
Swift
Turbo
Zippy

Slow

    Creeping
Dawdling
Delayed
Deliberate
Lagging
Languid
Leisurely
Loitering
Measured

Plodding
Pokey
Sluggish
Steady
Tardy

Strength

Strong

Beefy
Brawny
Burly
Hearty
Husky
Invincible
Mighty
Powerful
Robust
Rugged
Sinewy
Strapping

Weak

Decrepit
Derelict
Faint
Feeble
Flimsy
Frail
Infirm
Wimpy

TASTE

Flavors

Acidic
Bitter
Bittersweet
Citrus
Earthy
Fishy
Fruity
Nutty
Salty
Savory
Smoky
Sour
Spicy
Sugary
Sweet
Tangy
Tart
Zesty

Pleasant

Appetizing
Delectable
Palatable
Scrumptious

Succulent
Tasty
Toothsome
Yummy

Unpleasant

Bland
Nauseating
Vapid

Temperature

Hot

Balmy
Blazing
Boiling
Burning
Scorched
Searing
Sizzling
Steaming
Stifling
Sultry
Sun-baked
Sweltering
Tropical

Mild

Lukewarm
Tepid

Cold

Arctic
Chilly
Freezing
Frigid

Frosty
Frozen
Icy
Nippy
Raw
Wintry

TEXTURE

Bubbly

Effervescent
Fizzy
Foamy
Frothy
Soapy
Sudsy
Whipped

Dull

Blunt
Rounded

Hard

Dense
Firm
Iron
Jelled
Rocky
Set
Solid
Stale
Stony
Unforgiving

Light

Airy
Breezy
Ethereal
Flaky
Fluffy
Powdery
Puffy

Liquid

Diluted
Juicy
Runny
Watery

Rough

Bumpy
Charred
Choppy
Crinkly
Crispy
Crumbly
Crunchy
Crusty
Fibrous
Itchy
Leathery
Lumpy

Matted
Ribbed
Rippled
Roasted
Sandpaper
Scratchy
Scruffy
Splintered
Toasted
Wavy
Woolen

Sharp

Barbed
Bristled
Jagged
Pointed
Prickly
Spiked
Spiny

Smooth

Flush
Glassy
Glazed
Glossy
Polished
Silky
Slick

Slippery
Waxy

Soft

Billowy
Cotton
Cozy
Cushy
Furry
Fuzzy
Hairy
Lush
Mushy
Plush
Spongy
Tender
Velvety

Sticky

Gooey
Gummy
Pasty
Slimy
Squishy

Worn

Decayed
Deteriorated

Frayed
Rusty
Shredded
Tattered
Weathered
Withered

Tightness

Loose

Baggy
Droopy
Floppy
Free
Hanging
Limp
Saggy
Slack

Tight

Airtight
Attached
Bound
Clasped
Compact
Constricted
Drawn
Hooked
Knitted
Knotted
Locked
Pinned
Pressed
Snug

Stuck
Taut
Tied
Wedged
Wound

WEIGHT

Heavy

> Burdensome
> Hefty
> Overweight
> Weighty

Light

> Feathery
> Floating
> Weightless

WETNESS

Dry

Arid
Chalky
Cracked
Dehydrated
Dusty
Sandy

Wet

Bathed
Clammy
Damp
Dank
Doused
Dripping
Foggy
Humid
Marshy
Misty
Moist
Muggy
Saturated
Soaked
Sopping
Steamy

Sweaty
Watery

OTHER HELPFUL
ADJECTIVES

_____

_____

_____

_____

_____

_____

_____

_____

_____

_____

_____

_____

_____

_____

About

VALERIE HOWARD has been a self-published author since 2011. She's a follower of Jesus, the wife of a pastor, the mother and teacher of two energetic boys, a graduate of Bible college, and the author of several novels, plays, non-fiction books, and children's books.

If you liked this book, you may also like:

1,000 Strong Verbs for Fiction Writers
1,000 Character Reactions from Head to Toe

(Both free with Kindle Unlimited)

Get a free book at ForIndieAuthors.com

www.Facebook.com/forindieauthors

www.Instagram.com/forindieauthors

Made in the USA
Monee, IL
14 December 2022

21567196R00039